A Pianist's A to Z

by the same author

THE VEIL OF ORDER
Conversations with Martin Meyer

ALFRED BRENDEL ON MUSIC
His Collected Essays

PLAYING THE HUMAN GAME
Collected Poems of Alfred Brendel

ALFRED BRENDEL

A Pianist's A to Z

A PIANO LOVER'S READER

English version by the author
with Michael Morley

Drawings by Gottfried Wiegand

ff
faber and faber

Originally published in 2012 in Germany as *A bis Z eines Pianisten: Ein Lesebuch für Klavierliebende* by Carl Hanser Verlag, Munich

First published in English in the UK in 2013
by Faber and Faber Limited
Bloomsbury House
74–77 Great Russell Street
London WC1B 3DA

Typeset by Faber and Faber Ltd
Printed and bound by CPI Group (UK) Ltd, Croydon, CR0 4YY

A CIP record for this book
is available from the British Library

ISBN 978–0–571–30184–3

FSC
www.fsc.org
MIX
Paper from responsible sources
FSC® C013604

4 6 8 10 9 7 5 3

PREFACE This book distils what, at my advanced age, I feel able to say about music, musicians, and matters of my pianistic profession. My other métier, literature, tells me to say things simply, but without undue simplification. Comprehensiveness is not an issue – my literary sympathies tend towards the fragment and the aphorism. Those readers who are unfamiliar with my essays (*Alfred Brendel on Music*) or my conversations with Martin Meyer (*The Veil of Order*, *Me of All People*) are invited to look for more copious information there.

One can succumb to music, as it were with closed eyes, and simply 'do' it. One can formalise it, intellectualise, poeticise, psychologise. One can deliver pronouncements, in sociological terms, on what music is allowed, or not allowed, to represent. One can infer from the pieces what they are or read into them what they should be. To the best of my ability I have sought to avoid the latter. An inclination for facing the music consciously, and linking it to the pleasures of language, has prevailed.

When talking about composers, I shall call them 'grand masters' where I feel that they show pre-eminence in certain forms or types of work. (My apologies to freemasons and chess players.) In my vocabulary, words like greatness, genius and mastery still have their rightful place.

No conclusions should be drawn from the fact that the composers to whom I allot entries do not extend into the twentieth century. The absence of appreciations of, say, Debussy and Ravel, Schoenberg, Bartók, Stravinsky, Messiaen and Ligeti is connected to the fact that my own repertoire has, to a large extent, belonged to a musical era steeped in cantabile. We may call it the golden age of piano composition. Much twentieth-century music subsequently abandoned cantabile as its core. My friends know how passionately I have followed the music of the last hundred years. I cannot admire enough the heroism of that handful of composers who dared to pursue the consequences of the dissolution of tonality around 1908–9. It may be worth mentioning that I have performed Schoenberg's Piano Concerto sixty-eight times on five continents. An examination of this work can be found among my essays.

The present book was completed under the friendly auspices of the Wissenschaftskolleg zu Berlin. Valuable information came from Monika Möllering, Till Fellner and Maria Majno. My special thanks go to my co-translator Michael Morley. I dedicate *A Pianist's A to Z* to my fellow musicians in admiration or amicable dissent, to my audiences in gratitude, and to the great composers in love.

A. B.

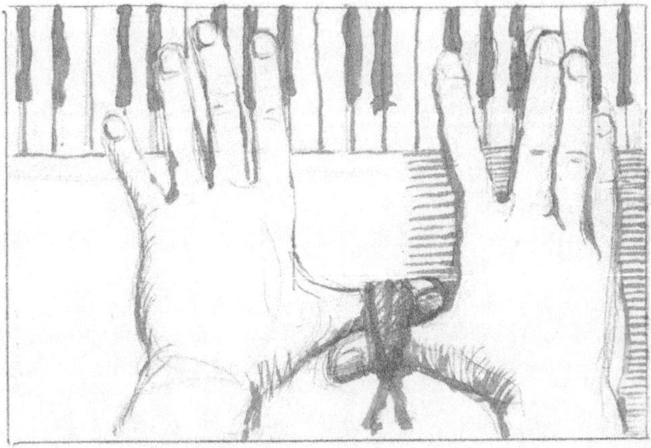

A

ACCENT If we want to see music as a landscape, accents would figure in it as hills and towers, humps and spires, planes and ravines. Unless accents are tied to syncopations they usually need to be prepared. Frequently the upbeat will take over part – in Schubert sometimes a large part – of their intensity. The opening rhythmic figure of Schubert's *Wanderer Fantasy* sounds, in this way, fresher and more natural; dactylic, it is marking time. Schubert was an accent enthusiast; it will often be necessary to translate his accents into a cantabile style. For a start, one has to distinguish his accent markings, sometimes excessively large in size, from diminuendo markings. The accented French horn notes at the beginning of the 'Great' C major Symphony should be gently highlighted in their entirety rather than stabbed.

In Beethoven, we encounter, next to the customary accent mark, various other prescriptions and graduations like *sforzando*, *sforzato*, *rinforzando*, *fortepiano* and multiple repeated *forte*. (See *Alfred Brendel on Music*, pp. 35–7.)

ARPEGGIO Not just a way of accommodating small hands, but a means of expression. The expressive range of arpeggios reaches from the vehement to the mysterious (e.g. the opening of Beethoven's Sonata Op. 31 No. 2).

It is easily forgotten that 'arpeggio' derives from *arpa* (harp). The pianist should envisage a lady harpist controlling the rhythm and dynamics of her arpeggios with her gracious fingertips. Arpeggios need attentive care and acute ears. Where the *arpeggiando* sign is not indicated as spread across both hands, we should be hearing two simultaneous harps.

ARRANGEMENT (ADAPTATION) In the baroque era, works of other composers used frequently to be adapted without naming the source. Bach's famous D minor *Toccata and Fugue* for organ may well be an adaptation of a work by a contemporary (if not by Bach himself), written for solo violin.

Where composers themselves suggest that the same work might be played by different instruments – like Schumann indicating either horn or cello – they are, to a certain extent, adapters of their own music. Heinz Holliger played chamber works by Schumann beautifully on his various oboes. Regrettably, a recording of Mozart arias which I had begged him to do never materialised.

There are different categories and degrees of adaptation. The most obvious is confined to ornamentation and supplementation in baroque music or Mozart. Then there are transcriptions from one medium into another (Liszt's 'piano scores' of Berlioz's *Symphonie fantastique*, of the Beethoven symphonies or Weber overtures), and those that make use of excerpts or elements of works, like Liszt's opera paraphrases, or modify the works in the personal manner of the transcriber. Liszt has cultivated all of these. To anyone eager to grasp the knack of turning the piano into an orchestra, or producing operatic singing in pianistic terms, Liszt's adaptations will provide incomparable enlightenment. Consulting the original scores, as well as good orchestral performances, should further sharpen the senses and help to find the exact reference point.

There were periods in which adaptations were welcome and obvious, and others where they were reviled. In justifying his free treatment of certain works, Busoni maintained that each notation of a work already amounts to a transcription – a point of view I cannot share. But I admire his imposing piano versions of organ works, which manage to reproduce, besides the sonorities of the instrument, the resonance of church acoustics.

Since the 1920s, the increasing number of *Urtext* editions has fuelled a new purism. Schoenberg, who expected the performer to be 'his most ardent servant', nevertheless produced orchestrations of late-Romantic opulence of Bach's E flat *Prelude and Fugue* for organ BWV 552 and Brahms's G minor Piano Quartet. Since the last decades of the twentieth century a new wave of adapting and transcribing has swept over us: composers have displayed a penchant for paraphrasing their own works (Berio) or for using older masterpieces as a testing ground for their own notions of sound and structure.

I would call myself neither an adversary of all adaptations nor a spokesman for constant adapting. But I cannot agree with an approach that views masterpieces merely as raw material for personal excursions, treating them the way some contemporary directors treat plays. Where additions are necessary and desirable they ought to blend with the style of the composer. In general, substantial post-baroque compositions have remained more convincing in their original form. (An exception: Weber's *Invitation to the Dance* in Berlioz's ravishing orchestration.) I sympathise with the pleasure derived from turning Schubert's *Wanderer Fantasy* or Mussorgsky's *Pictures from an Exhibition* into an orchestral score; yet for me, the original text clearly wins, all the more so since our present pianos have given us the chance of transforming the sound into an orchestra more colourfully than ever.

ART AND ARTISTS There are those who believe that delving into the biography of artists ensures a deeper perception of their art. I am not one of them. The notion that a work of art has to mirror the person of the artist, that man and work are an equation, that the integrity of the person proves the integrity of his production – such belief seems to me to belong, particularly in the area of music, to the realm of wishful thinking. (The poet Christian Morgenstern has his hero Palmström assert that 'there cannot be what must not be'.)

Beethoven's frequently chaotic handwriting in his letters and musical autographs reminds us of his domestic disarray as we know it from pictures and descriptions. In complete contrast, there is the enduring order of his compositions.

The person of a great composer and his work remain to me incommensurable: a human being with its limitations facing a well-nigh limitless musical universe.

There are exceptional cases where events from the composer's life can be traced in the music. Beethoven, in his Sonata Op. 110, composed the experience of returning to life after a severe case of jaundice. Similarly, Schoenberg in his String Trio turned a major health crisis into sound. And Brahms conceived his D minor Piano Concerto under the impact of Schumann's plunge into the Rhine.

Generally, however, the desire to link tendencies and incidents in an artist's life to his compositions will lead us astray. The notion that a griever longs to compose his grief, a dying musician the experience of dying or a person overwhelmed with joy his gaiety, belongs in the realm of fairy tales. Music is full of counter-examples. Works of happiness, joyfulness, serenity, and even lightness have emerged from periods of great personal distress. Let us rejoice at that.

B

BACH When Beethoven exclaimed that to do him justice, the master's name should have been not *Bach* (brook) but *Meer* (the sea), he spoke not only of the surpassing abundance and diversity of more than a thousand compositions but also of the creative power embodied in this supreme exponent of the most widely extended family of professional musicians ever.

I see Johann Sebastian Bach as the grand master of music for all keyboard instruments: the initiator of the piano concerto, the creator of the *Goldberg Variations*, the master of the solo suite and partita, of chorale preludes, fugues, and cantatas. When, in the post-war years, Bach's piano works were assigned exclusively to the harpsichord or clavichord, young pianists were deprived of the main source of polyphonic playing. To most of us, the assumption that Bach doesn't fit with the modern piano is outmoded. On present-day instruments one can individualise each voice and give plasticity to the contrapuntal progress of a fugue. The playing can be orchestral, atmospheric and colourful, and the piano can sing. To restrict a composer who was himself one of the most resolute transcribers of works by himself and others in this way might seem misguided even to practitioners of 'historical performance'.

Alongside the boundless wealth of Bachian counterpoint the free-roaming creator of fantasies and toccatas must not be forgotten. In the spectacular A minor Fantasy ('Prelude') BWV 922, to give just one example, no bar reveals where the next one will go.

Since the second half of the twentieth century something miraculous has happened: the complementary figure of George Frederic Handel has re-emerged. The opportunity to familiarise myself with a multitude of Handel's works has been, for me, one of the greatest gifts. The drama of his operas and oratorios, his vocal invention (by no means inferior to Mozart's or Schubert's), the fire of his coloratura and his characteristic clarity and generosity now place him beside Bach as a figure comparable in stature.

BALANCE A crucial element of sound. No matter how relaxed and physically natural the performer's approach may be, the result will be found wanting if chords and vertical sound combinations remain undifferentiated or when the balancing is left to the instrument. Common defects include: the concept of equally loud playing from both hands; a lack of attention to part-writing; and the permanent stressing of upper voice and bass. The fifth finger of the left hand can sound as if made of steel, and octaves in the bass register are sometimes allowed to drown out the rest. Of course there are pianos whose bass is overly loud; some time ago this used to be standard practice in America. Even more frequent is the dominance of the lower middle range, particularly when the soft pedal is applied. But the player should not accept the shortcomings of an inadequately voiced instrument as God-given. The bass should, in my opinion, be highlighted only when it has something special to say. The upper half of the piano should sing and be luminous, while the lower should dominate only in exceptional cases. The player's arms ought, where necessary, to be as independent of one another as if they belonged to different beings.

Balancing suggests terraces and distances, colour and character, darkness and light. Rather than bass-heavy players, I prefer those who enable the music to leave the ground and float.

BEETHOVEN Grand master of chamber music, sonata, variation and symphony.

What other composer has covered, within his life, such vast musical distances? We pianists are fortunate to have the chance to follow the path of his thirty-two piano sonatas all the way to his late quartets, supplemented by the cosmos of his *Diabelli Variations*, and the *Bagatelles* Op. 126. A distillation of his development is presented by the five Piano–Cello Sonatas.

Who else offers the range from comedy to tragedy, from the lightness of many of his variation works to the forces of nature that he not only unleashed but held in check? And which master managed, as Beethoven did in his late music, to weld together present, past and future, the sublime and the profane?

Some prejudices have prevailed: the image of a thoroughly heroic Beethoven, or of a Beethoven who, in his late works, has become downright esoteric. Let's remember that he could be graceful in his own personal way, and that his *dolce*, his warmth and tenderness are no less a feature of his music than vehemence and high spirits.

BEGINNING The pianist appears on stage, sits down, fidgets around on his chair and alters its height, opens and shuts his eyes, repeatedly places his fingers on the keys, grabs his knees, and, after an inner push, finally starts playing. Why not try out the piano, and the piano stool, beforehand, and start without fuss?

The beginning of a work usually establishes its basic character. In a good performance, it should be conveyed right away. The performer needs to acquire the skill to communicate it with assurance.

BRAHMS Brahms was a pianist who in his early days did not hesitate to present, in a concert, an operatic paraphrase by Thalberg. I like to imagine him seated at the piano, short but handsome, at the Schumanns. The combination of technical bravura with rootedness in the music of Bach and Beethoven and a touch of Kapellmeister–Kreisler romanticism must have electrified Robert and Clara. An inclination towards virtuosity and the presentation of new and prodigious technical hurdles remained a hallmark of at least part of his pianistic output. In this, as well as in a recurring predilection for Hungarian gypsiness, one can detect a kinship with his older musical counterpart, Franz Liszt.

In the D minor Concerto, considered to be a reaction to the outbreak of Schumann's insanity and reworked in several versions, Brahms created the most monumental symphonic work for piano and orchestra. Its grandeur, heroic as well as moving, is still free from a proliferation of parallel thirds and sixths, but it also avoids an over-abundance of polyrhythmic complexities. When the young composer played the work in Leipzig's Gewandhaus he seemed to have been fairly happy with himself. However the audience hissed. It is easy to assume that his listeners would have had some trouble taking in the solo part at all – on the pianos of his day even such athletic piano writing would, next to the orchestra, have had virtually no chance.

With all my admiration for the later variations, rhapsodies, intermezzi and piano quartets, and with a respectful bow towards the huge symphonic-chamber hybrid of the B flat Concerto, the purest Brahms remains for me the one between the first Piano Trio and the first String Sextet. To it, and particularly to the D minor Concerto, goes my love.

C

CANTABILE Bach wrote his Two-Part Inventions and Three-Part Symphonies expressly as pieces for instruction in the art of cantabile playing. Until the twentieth century, the singing line was at the heart of music. The piano can indeed sing – if the pianist wants to make it sing and knows how to do it. Singers, string players, oboists should be our models. But continuous legato playing is not the secret of cantabile; the music has to speak as well. Melodic phrases have to be articulated, and the pedal is entitled to play a connecting and ennobling role. Beauty and warmth of the cantilena ought to be a player's innermost need.

The modern piano, as long as the quality of its sound is not overly short and strident, offers greater opportunities to play in a singing fashion than either harpsichords or the hammerklavier. Listen to Edwin Fischer's recording of the second movement of Bach's F minor Concerto!

CHARACTER There are formalists who think that form and structure are the Alpha and Omega of music. For me, it has always been the dualism of form and psychology, structure and character, intellect and feeling, that determines music-making. It is erroneous to think that the perception of form and structure will automatically reveal the character, the atmosphere, the psychological condition of a piece. We have here two forces that work together and on each other, but not in the sense of an equation. On the other hand, musicians who entirely rely on their emotions, be warned: even if we acknowledge feeling as the starting-point and goal of music, we shouldn't forget that only the control, the filter of the intellect makes a work of art possible. Chaos has to be turned into order.

Couperin had written 'character pieces'. C. P. E. Bach spoke of 'affects', Rousseau and Schoenberg of 'expression'. In a performace of a Beethoven sonata, the grasp of its character, or characters, will be just as crucial as the representation of its compositional shape.

CHOPIN At one with the piano, Chopin remains the ruler in the domains of the etude, the mazurka and the polonaise, the master of ballades, scherzos and impromptus, but above all of the twenty-four Preludes, one of the peaks of all piano music. It is hard to comprehend that Busoni is said to have been the first important virtuoso to play the Preludes as a cycle – all the more so as Busoni did not belong to the club of Chopin specialists. There will be few today who remember that, until the middle of the twentieth century, performing Chopin was mainly the domain of 'the Chopin player'.

There were good reasons for it. With the exception of a few works, Chopin wrote exclusively for the piano. He loved great singing but didn't leave us one truly successful song. The direct connection to ensemble rhythm, to the colours of the orchestra and the timbres of other instruments, is consequently missing; for other major piano composers it was quite natural. A large part of their musical imagination never lost touch with these other areas, while Chopin drew his inspiration primarily, if not exclusively, from his instrument. It is, therefore, hardly surprising that he developed a highly personal style of performance, which fitted his own music while being inappropriate to the music of others. Chopin's music claimed the performer root and branch. Meanwhile Chopin, the bird of paradise, has been swallowed up by the musical mainstream.

Where is the player who, somewhere between the extremes of conservatory and coffee house, is able to find the poetic core of this music? Ironically, Chopin, unlike Schumann and Liszt, hardly mentioned 'poetry' at all.

CHORD A conductor once lectured me: 'If a pianist plays all the notes of a chord equally loudly, then he demonstrates a good technique.' No wonder his conducting lacked warmth and refinement.

Be aware of the middle voices. Chords can be illuminated from within.

COHESION In one of his films, Charlie Chaplin is the assistant of a pawnbroker. When a client brings an alarm clock Chaplin dismantles it in front of his eyes until all its components are spread out in front of him. Then he sweeps the lot into the owner's hat.

Let us now envisage a watchmaker who puts a clock together. He knows that each cog-wheel, each spring is part of the whole. One thing needs the other. Only in assembling them (composition) can the clock embark on its life: ticking, showing the time, and rousing the sleeper.

Let us now forget the watchmaker and his creation altogether, as illuminating as they may be, and think of a plant unfolding or a creature made out of clay that starts breathing and pulsating, a living being whose heartbeat ensures continuity, and whose breath, far beyond the natural breath of a singer, holds the work together in one great arc. To produce this arc is our supreme task. By showing how a composer has been able to lead us convincingly from the first note to the last, we demonstrate his stature.

COMPOSER Without composers there would be no performance. And without the work that becomes, as an autonomous creation, independent of the composer to a certain degree, there would be no source of information for the player. It tells us what is to be done, if not always with exhaustive clarity and completeness.

I am not speaking here of slavish subservience or the mentality of the parade-ground. We should help the composer to the best of our abilities and do it of our own free will. But we had better not presume to be the composer's governess or the saviour of pieces that crave to be elevated by superior insight.

Young pianists would be well advised to find a composition teacher and compose themselves, at least for a while. The experience of inventing and writing down music, of organising pieces and carrying them through from the first note to the last, will perhaps enable us to perceive a composer's notation in a different light and with different respect. What is the meaning of this *forte* marking? Why did he write a crotchet and not a quaver? Could the reason have been carelessness? (Such things do happen, as in the Rondo of Beethoven's G major Concerto.) A spell of composing experience, even if transitory, will leave its mark on the player's future judgement of works. The question 'How is this piece composed?' will be of benefit in dealing with the other, more customary one: 'How should this work be played?'

CONCERTO There are concert pianists who feel most comfortable when they are alone with the public. They get all the attention. Then there is the musical partner, happy to have company and a raised stand on the piano with music on it. The genre of the piano concerto combines these two types. The soloist has to dominate yet, at times, be sufficiently discreet, in chamber-music fashion. Between these two positions Mozart's piano concertos lie roughly in the middle. As a body of works they have remained, at least from K271 on, a veritable wonder of the world. Their range extends from the most personal – D minor (K466), C minor (K491) – to the most official, in C major (K503). Beethoven went on from there. His five concertos strike me as sharply characterised individuals, which makes them eminently suitable for performance as a cycle. One could jokingly, and in reverse familial chronology, speak of two very lively teenagers (B flat and C major), a young man (C minor) with a strongly pronounced inner life (in E major!), and their parents (G major – mother, E flat – father). In spite of the glory of subsequent piano concertos, such classic flights of excellence have hardly been equalled. But the species itself has remained very much alive – as the works of Schoenberg, Bartók, Prokofiev, Messiaen (*Oiseaux exotiques*) or Ligeti impressively demonstrate.

In the works of J. S. Bach, the arch-founder of the piano concerto, there occurs a splendid fully fledged cadenza, namely that of the Fifth Brandenburg Concerto. It is 'through-composed', while classical cadenzas subsequently became, or feigned to be, improvisations. They now lead by detour from the six-four chord to the tutti of the orchestra. Mozart's many original cadenzas never seriously depart from the basic tonality! Anyone who supplies cadenzas where Mozart didn't leave his own should respect this important feature. The next generation started the daredevil game of modulating anywhere and everywhere: cadenzas became areas for flights of fancy. They explode the character of the movement and wreck classical conventions left and right. Beethoven, in his giant cadenza for his C major Concerto, cheerfully runs amok.

CONDUCTOR Watching singers and conductors is, for the pianist, the most important source of learning. While the singer reminds us of the need to sing as well as to speak, the conductor offers us the orchestra as a model of balance, colour and rhythm. (The image of the pianist as a ten-fingered orchestra seems to originate with Hans von Bülow.) Our tempo modifications should be 'conductable' as long as the piece doesn't demand an improvisatory approach. In our mind, we conduct ourselves! Next to the rhythmic recklessness of some all-too-soloistic players, ensemble rhythm serves as a corrective.

In piano concertos, most conductors will try to be helpful as long as the pianist has a precise concept of the whole piece and doesn't ask for the absurd and impossible. The soloist's ideas need to be relayed in advance. There are, however, conductors who indicate, after having been told three things: 'Don't tell me a fourth; I won't remember it anyway.'

CONTROL Since the advent of good recording, musicians have improved their ability to listen to themselves. They can now take in, as it were from the outside, what they do to compositions, a gain not to be despised. Along the way, there has also been a gain in the accuracy of musical intentions, fortified by the growing number of *Urtext* editions. There is no doubt that, in extreme cases, excessive control can lead to pedantry. But shouldn't greater awareness and acuteness rather bring about an enhanced sense of wonder? I side with Robert Musil who proposed the idea of a 'central office for accuracy and soul' in his great fragment of a novel, *The Man Without Qualities*.

COUGHING In Chicago, I stopped during a very soft piece and told the public: 'I can hear you but you can't hear me.' For the rest of the recital, nobody stirred. Have you noticed that in a fine hall the perception of music is good almost anywhere – as long as you don't sit right next to the brass? The same applies to coughing, sneezing, clearing one's throat, rustling, clicking the tongue, or babbling. If you really can't help coughing, be sure to do so during soft passages and general pauses: the 'Coughing Rhinemaiden', a tag worn dangling around your neck, will be handed to you in due course by one of the ushers.

P.S. – during funny pieces, laughing is permitted.

CRESCENDO Can be played in one even stretch, or in waves, or with a sudden bend upwards. The bend gives the crescendo a special voltage. Within a crescendo that leads to a big climax, the sound should become wider and not more pointed.

In Beethoven, *crescendi* are usually indicated with amazing precision; they start precisely where the word is written and not in the next bar, or even later. (It took me quite a while to realise this.) Hans von Bülow's popular dictum, 'crescendo means piano, diminuendo forte' – suggesting that each crescendo must start softly enough, and each diminuendo begin loudly enough to be effective – is misleading in its exaggeration, although it may be necessary to start a crescendo on a lower level if it occurs within a *forte* passage.

D

DANCE For many cultures, music and dance are inseparable. Beyond the suites and partitas of the baroque era, dance and dancing have remained an important element of music well into the twentieth century. There have even been musicians who insist that the essence of all music is dance. I personally wouldn't like to go that far lest a *Credo* or *Dies irae* may turn out to be skipping along.

Where we frequently have to think and feel in terms of dancing is in minuets, scherzos and finales. All final movements of Beethoven's concertos dance. For the player this means that the listener, in his imagination, should feel the urge to dance along, inspired by a rhythm that, as it were, celebrates itself and irresistibly takes possession of the dancers' bodies.

DEPTH What I have in mind is not depth of feeling but spatial, three-dimensional depth. Sound can be flat or spatial. A performance may sound two- or three-dimensional or suggest the plasticity of contour in relief. It can simultaneously present not only a number of colours but also a number of distances. Bernard Berenson, talking about paintings, coined the term 'tactile values'. Even more gratifying is the notion of a piece of music as a three-dimensional object one can wander around.

DIMINUENDO There are musicians who habitually and tirelessly produce diminuendos on two-note groups, repeated notes, ends of phrases and even ends of pieces. In some present-day performances, works of the baroque or classical era sound as if they had been composed to celebrate a diminuendo cult. I have heard singers who soften each phrase-ending no matter what the harmony or text may suggest. Similarly, in a pair of energetic chords the second chord tends to be softened. Notwithstanding the delight I take in declamation, exaggeration of the telling detail can lead to mannerism. Coherence, the through-line, attention to sequential links, remain, for me, essential.

DIVERSITY Great music is a series of exceptional cases. Each masterpiece adds something new to musical experience. Wagner's request – 'Children, produce something new! New! And again: new!' – has, in my assessment, kept its decisive significance. However, this diversity should, in performance, be generated not by the performer's caprice but by the requirements of the work itself. Stereotypes of declamation and articulation obstruct such requirements.

What makes a work singular? The first movement of Beethoven's G major Concerto contains three brief lyrical episodes, each of them appearing only once, like phenomenal glimpses of another sphere. How are they to be fittingly accommodated within a performance?

Why does Beethoven's Sonata Op. 110 strike us as unprecedented and surprising? The immediate succession of a lyrical *amabile*, of burlesque profanity ('I am dissolute, you are dissolute, we are all dissolute people'), and intertwined baroque forms dependent on a psychological programme, is unique.

In twenty-four mostly terse character pieces, Chopin's Preludes traverse all the keys. Unlike the pieces within a cycle of variations, each Prelude has its own independent face. Distinct characterisation and rapid readjustment are required. Listen to Alfred Cortot's incomparable recording from 1933–4! Only a performance of all the Preludes in succession will reveal their magnificent richness and unfailing craftsmanship.

DOLCE A famous visiting conductor once said to the string players of a German orchestra during a rehearsal of Mozart's piano concerto K595: '*Meine Herren, spielen Sie dolce! Dolce ist süß.*' (Gentleman, play *dolce*! *Dolce* means sweet!) Forty years ago, orchestras consisted almost exclusively of men. Another well-known musician confessed to me that, when facing Beethoven's *dolce*, he was all at sea. 'What on earth does he mean?'

He wasn't the only one to ask. 'Sweet', however, doesn't get us very far. 'Tender', an Italian meaning of the word, is more helpful. But in Beethoven's *dolce*, there is also warmth and introspection. While *espressivo* is directed more to the outside, *dolce* aims inward. The German *innig* comes nearest. Warmth, tenderness, introspection are important hallmarks of Beethoven's lyricism. These days they have become a rarity.

E

EMOTION (FEELING) 'In human beings, there is a dangerous amalgam of intellect and emotion' (Max Born to Albert Einstein). In a great work of art, the mix should be felicitous and uplifting.

The lovely term 'emotional distinctness' (*Gefühlsdeutlichkeit*) was coined by Robert Schumann. There is also such a thing as emotional quality control. It is impressively demonstrated by Beethoven as long as he was not succumbing to composing works like *Der glorreiche Augenblick* or *Wellingtons Sieg*. We find first-, second- and third-hand emotions, emotions for teenagers, grown-ups and senior citizens. There is also kitsch, an emotional tangle of particular tenacity.

Someone asked Artur Schnabel: 'Do you play with feeling or in time?' Schnabel replied: 'Why shouldn't I be feeling in time?' The assumption that feeling and anarchy of tempo are causally linked continues to obscure some minds.

Hans von Bülow distinguished between feeling (*Gefühl*) and doziness (*Dusel*).

A joke, possibly originating with Busoni, posed the question: 'What is the difference between Leopold Godowsky and a pianola?' The answer: 'Godowsky plays twice as fast as a pianola while a pianola is twice as emotional as Godowsky.'

'If feeling does not prompt, in vain you strive' (Goethe, *Faust* I).

ENDINGS The end of a piece reaches the borders of silence. Endings can bring the piece to a close, but also, in some cases, unlock silence. This happens in Beethoven's Opp. 109 and 111. The Sonata Op. 110 does something different: it liberates itself from musical shackles in a kind of euphoric self-immolation. The end of Liszt's B minor Sonata leads back into the silence of its beginning.

There are many kinds of endings – triumphant and tragic, poetic and laconic, funny and melancholic, majestic and expiring. We find endings that present a final conclusion and others that leave things open. Open endings, as in Schumann's 'Kind im Einschlummern' or Liszt's 'Unstern' (Disaster) point into the unknown and the mysterious, unseal an enigma.

ENSEMBLE Nearly all great composers for the piano have also been, if not principally, composers for ensemble. Chopin, who hardly wrote any ensemble music, is the great exception. These days, performances of Beethoven's quartets are, on the whole, more rewarding than those of his piano sonatas. Why?

Because the rhythm of four musicians needs to be coordinated. But they also have to agree about the details of their execution. The composer's markings give them a matching orientation. They don't lose themselves in the whim of the moment – or at least they take their liberties within certain confines. The pianist who complains about having to wear a rhythmic corset while playing with others should reconsider his habits.

EXTREMES There are extremists of tempo; they play fast things even faster and slow things even slower than ordinary mortals. There are also extremists of volume; between the softest and the loudest, the musical landscape lies fallow. Let's cultivate the intermediate space! The whole gamut of dynamics, the whole diversity of tempi should be at our command. Extremes should be deployed only where the music really calls for them.

F

FANTASY It would be a mistake, in classical and Romantic Fantasies, to view the improvisational aspect as the principal feature. Fantasies can be rigorously 'through-composed' even if 'peculiarity, immediacy and freedom' (Riemann) are their distinguishing characteristics. What they have in common is that they do not fit the familiar canon of forms. The four sections of Schubert's *Wanderer Fantasy* eschew conventional sonata form. Its first section presents a sonata form that merely extends to the development section; the development is replaced by an Adagio with variations while the scherzo feigns a kind of recapitulation in the 'wrong key' of A flat major; finally the fugato of the coda reaffirms as the proper recapitulation the initial key of C major. Rhapsodic looseness is not what this work or Mozart's marvellous C minor Fantasy K475 are aiming at – rather originality of form and structure. Bach's *Chromatic Fantasy*, on the other hand, is a written-down improvisation, seemingly spontaneous and endlessly surprising.

To the Romantics, Fantasies represented a formal ideal. Each piece should find its own shape. In this uniqueness, classical forms are absorbed or revoked.

FIDELITY TO THE LETTER Are we expected to play what the composer has put on paper? The answer should be: as extensively as possible. There is a stress on 'possible'. Blind trust can go too far. In autographs and early editions, there may be errors and inaccuracies. Besides asking 'What did the composer intend to write down?' we should also deal with the questions 'What did he mean to convey?' and 'How can we do justice to the demands of the piece?' The text alone is not the full message.

In the case of the so-called 'Moonlight' Sonata, the indication at its beginning, *sempre pp e senza sordino*, suggests continuous use of the pedal – but not, of course, in one huge blur. In his comments on the performance of Beethoven's piano works, his pupil Carl Czerny explains that the pedal should be changed with each bass note, i.e. with each new harmony. Czerny, with all due caution, remains an important source of information on Beethoven playing.

On instruments of Beethoven's time, the execution of octave glissandos like those in the Prestissimo of the 'Waldstein' Sonata was perfectly feasible thanks to their shallower action and the availability of the so-called *Pianozug*, a pedal that reduced the sound to a ghostly whisper. It is crucial that these octaves should whisk by in *pianissimo*. On today's pianos, however, they can sound intrusively substantial unless they are done with two hands. Glissandos can be convincingly imitated.

The initial, somewhat risky leaps in Beethoven's 'Hammerklavier' Sonata Op. 106 are written in the lower system, yet they can be played with the help of the right hand. It is, to me, mysterious why some pianists resist doing so. Uniquely in Beethoven's sonatas, the work starts *ff*. When both hands are used, the sound will be more warmly powerful, and better controlled. Does the character of this opening really gain from physical risk? And can daring only be conveyed with one hand? What kind of daring would be musically appropriate anyway – a daring that would undermine rhythmic equilibrium and unsettle the upbeat? No orchestra would play this very orchestral beginning in such a way. Furthermore, there is a fiery Allegro to deal with, even if we only play minim = 120 instead of Beethoven's 138. Also, the initial rhythm is one of the basic motives of the piece. Instead of blindly accepting how the composer distributed the notes between the hands, the player should imagine what sound is necessary, and how it can be produced.

In the opening movement of the A major Sonata Op. 2 No. 2, we face a situation that is downright absurd. The famous right-hand passages in bars 84–5 and 88–9 are provided with nonsensical fingerings unplayable even by fanatics of literalness. Beethoven the practical joker?

FINGERING I know pianists who have succumbed to the habit of writing, into their scores, the requisite fingering for each note. In contrast, Paul Hindemith famously declared at the beginning of his *Suite '1922'*: 'Don't waste your time deciding whether to play G sharp with the fourth or sixth finger.'

Into a copy of Bach's Cello Suites, Rudolf von Tobel, Pablo Casals' assistant at the masterclasses in Zermatt, entered every fingering that Casals ever played: the figures piled up three or four high above the notes.

In complicated pieces it will be advisable for the player, unlike the great Casals, to stick to those fingerings that are clinging to his motoric memory. Anyone who has practised the fugue of Beethoven's Op. 106 early on will be well advised not to alter his fingerings substantially. There is the very real danger that deeper layers of memory may surface again and confuse the player during a concert.

There are fingerings for normal mortals, and those devised by great pianists. The fingerings of Bülow, d'Albert or Schnabel show distinct personality. For me, Bülow's change of fingers in the repeated notes of the Scherzo from Beethoven's 'Hammerklavier' Sonata proved to be of lasting benefit. Despite critical reservations, Bülow's editions of Beethoven's late sonatas and *Diabelli Variations* have remained stimulating.

Meanwhile, a new relationship between fingers and keys has been revealed in the drawings of Gottfried Wiegand (1926–2005).

FORM According to Hugo Riemann, form is unity in diversity. Aestheticians shortly before 1800 had applied the same formula to musical character.

To me, form and character (feeling, psychology, atmosphere, 'expression', 'impulse') are non-identical twins. The form and structure of a piece are visible and verifiable in the composer's text. The other twin has to be experienced. The visibility of form leads some to see the invisible twin as its subordinate. It is relatively simple to analyse a composition with the help of the written text, more difficult to feel the form, and even more demanding to enter into the psychology of a work.

G

GORGEOUS In Los Angeles, a lady greeted me after a concert and implored me to arrange Wagner operas for piano and orchestra. In her day, she had been a well-known coloratura soprano. An LP record with a colourful sleeve bore the title *Miliza Korjus – Rhymes with Gorgeous.*

H

HARMONY If we decide to call singing the heart of music – at least of the music of the past – what then is harmony? The third dimension, the body, the space, the mesh of nerves, the tension within the tonal order, but also the tension in the apparent no man's land of the post-tonal. The performer is expected to reveal such tensions right into their tiniest ramifications. Transitions, transformations, changes of musical climate, and surprises all resist calculation. We need to feel them. I prefer *playing* harmonic events to *explaining* them.

HUMOUR Can music be funny, comical, humorous on its own, without the help of the word or the stage? My answer is yes. Only the comic intent makes works like Haydn's late C major Sonata, Beethoven's Op. 31 No. 1, or, I would maintain, his *Diabelli* and *Eroica Variations* plausible. To introduce humour into absolute music was one of Haydn's great achievements. According to Georg August Griesinger, Haydn was able 'to lure the listener into the highest degree of the comical by frivolous twists and turns of the seemingly serious'. To Beethoven, the sublime was no less readily available than its opposite. (The German novelist Jean Paul called humour 'the sublime in reverse'.) While Mozart realised his feeling for humour in opera, Haydn and Beethoven practised it by contravening classical order. To the Romantics, order was no longer a given; they had to discover or create it in themselves. Grotesque comedy is provided, in twentieth-century music, by Ligeti and Kagel.

The problem with the comical is that it can be perceived very differently – or not at all. Music has been granted the ability to sigh but not to laugh. Some people deem themselves to be above laughter and consider earnestness a proof of human maturity. The old hierarchy of aesthetics that positioned tragedy at the top and comedy at the bottom still holds some in its thrall.

'Once in a while, I laugh, jest, play, am human' (Pliny the Younger).

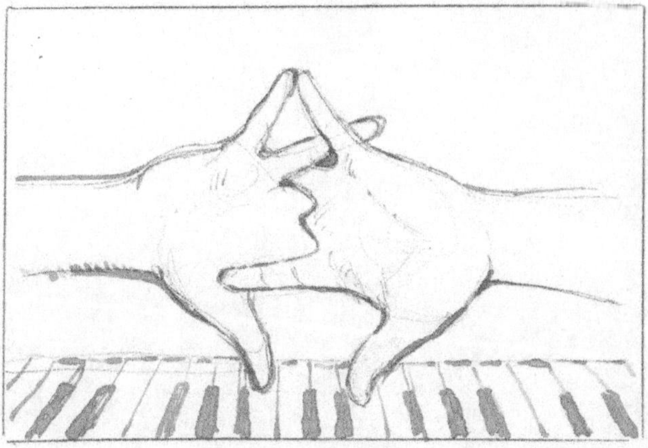

I

IDEAL The perfect blend of control and insight, of pulse and flexibility, of the expected and the unexpected – is it utopian to hope for this? After thorough preparation, the ideal performance may be around the corner, or so it seems. Let's leave open the possibility that there might at least be moments or minutes when the right wind stirs the strings of the Aeolian harp. The performer, as if by chance, arrives at a superior truth. With uncanny immediacy, our heart is touched. Listen to Edwin Fischer's playing of the coda of the Andante of Mozart's Concerto K482.

J

JEST The Austrian Emperor Joseph II did not enjoy Haydn's 'jests'. Plato wanted to ban laughter. There are people for whom sense, seriousness and accountability are everything: to laugh, they feel, is to make oneself ridiculous. Some of us listen to music as if all of it was written for the church. Test your sense of comedy in the face of Beethoven's *Diabelli Variations*.

Recently, an eminent biologist said: 'If you cannot laugh at life, then how in hell are you going to laugh at death?' Let us keep a few laughs for the end.

K

KLUNZ Jakob Klunz embodies the tragic case of a composer living at the wrong place at the wrong time. Under the relentless regime of Bismarck he was considered out of step when writing 389 waltzes for two to six hands. Imprisoned, he was coerced to compose his *Marches to Fail Victory*, posthumously published in a version for wind ensemble by Mauricio Kagel. The waltzes were sent anonymously, as a gesture of abasement, to the Austrian Emperor. To make things worse, they were subsequently destroyed by the Strauss family.

L

LEGATO I quote from Leopold Mozart's *Violin School*:

A singer who would separate each little figure, breathe in, and stress this or that little note would cause irrepressible laughter. The human voice connects one note with the next in the most unforced way . . . And who doesn't know that vocal music should always be what every instrumentalist has to keep in mind – because one needs, in all pieces, to come as close to being as natural as possible. One should therefore, where the singableness of a piece does not call for separations, aim to leave the bow on the violin in order to connect one bowing properly with the next. (V, 14)

On the piano as well, cantabile playing calls for an intense connection of the notes. But the pianist need not solely depend on finger-legato or *legatissimo*. Cohesion of sound can also be achieved with the pedal.

(*See* CANTABILE.)

LIED (SONG) Lieder like those of Schubert have opened up a new dimension to piano literature. The piano part now makes it tangibly clear that 'music can express everything'. Liszt has carried on from here. The player will deduce from the composed poems what has fired the pianistic characterisation. Singers, on the other hand, will find dynamic markings written down almost exclusively in the piano part. These days, one can expect that they have made themselves familiar with it.

Which had not always been the case. When we listen to collections of historical Schubert, Schumann or Wolf recordings we get the impression that the participation of the pianist was only barely tolerated. Interludes are rendered almost apologetically, and this happened even when a musical celebrity like Arthur Nikisch put himself at the service of Elena Gerhardt. Professional accompanists must have been obliging people who coached the singers to retain the notes, patiently accommodated their whims, shoved them into the right train, transposed by sight, and excelled in telling jokes.

From the 1930s onwards, musicians such as Gerald Moore in England and Michael Raucheisen in Germany brought about a gradual change. The focus is now on the unity of words and music, of voice and piano. But the singer is still in the forefront, the piano lid still on half-stick. Thanks to Dietrich Fischer-Dieskau the picture changed again: the accompanist now mutates into a partner. Increasingly, Fischer-Dieskau favoured piano soloists to sing with. Anyone who worked with him understood that he not only 'knew' the repertory phenomenally well, but was also able and willing to listen to the pianist and react to him.

In the early days of my dealings with Hermann Prey, he might sometimes hiss at me between two songs: 'You are too loud!' During my first rehearsal with Fischer-Dieskau, by contrast, he told me: 'You can give more.' And Mathias Goerne even invited me to open up the lid completely, a request I did not comply with. In this era of frequent live recordings, Lieder recitals are routinely played with a wide-open lid at the request of sound engineers. In the concert hall, this can easily create the impression that the singer is inside the piano rather than in front of it. I still belong among those musicians whose desire is that, in Lieder singing, the word, the plasticity of diction, the meaning of the text, the poem itself should reach the listener as directly as possible.

Richard Wagner said that, in his operas, it was not a question of passages either being sung or declaimed; rather, declamation was singing and singing declamation. This is just as valid for most songs. But even the solo pianist should never lose awareness of the fusion of singing and speaking – if not in the manner of those jokers who invent funny words to fit a tune.

LISZT Romantic sovereign of the piano. Creator of the religious piano piece. Chronicler of musical pilgrimages. Ceaseless practitioner of transcriptions and paraphrases. Radical precursor of modernity. Musical source of César Franck and Scriabin, Debussy and Ravel, Messiaen and Ligeti.

Familiarity with Liszt's piano works will make it evident that he was the piano's supreme artist. What I have in mind is not his transcendental pianistic skill but the reach of his expressive power. He, and only he, as a 'genius of expression' (Schumann), revealed the full horizon of what the piano was able to offer. Within this context, the pedal became a tool of paramount importance.

Liszt's uncertain standing as a composer can be traced back to a number of reasons: the variable quality of his works (with few exceptions, his finest achievements can be found in his piano music); the stylistic panorama of his compositions, which shows the influence of German and French music, Italian opera, the Hungarian gypsy manner, and Gregorian chant; and finally the fact that Liszt's music is dependent like no other on the quality of the performance. To use an aphorism by Friedrich Hebbel, music here 'only becomes visible when the correct gaze is focused on the writing'.

Liszt's outstanding piano works – among which I would like to mention only the B minor Sonata, *Années de pélérinage*, the *Variations on 'Weinen, Klagen, Sorgen, Zagen'*, *La lugubre gondola* and the finest of the Etudes – are for me on a par with those of Chopin and Schumann. His B minor Sonata surpasses, in originality, boldness and expressive range, anything written in this genre since Beethoven and Schubert.

According to Lina Ramann, his first biographer, we should see Liszt above all as a lyrical tone poet, 'rhetorician, rhapsodist, and mime'. She demands from the Liszt player 'the grand style', inwardness (*Innerlichkeit*), and passion. In a work like 'Vallée d'Obermann', all these qualities are evident. The improvisatory arbitrariness often associated with Liszt is contradicted by accounts of his playing in later years. It seems to me of crucial importance that, over a period of twelve years, Liszt remained in close contact with the Weimar orchestra as its principal conductor. A work like the B minor Sonata needs to be perceived in this context. Leo Weiner's remarkable orchestration of the Sonata can provide more essential information for the performer than the urge to whip up a succession of feverish dreams. With their metronome markings, both the *Liszt-Pädagogium* and Siloti's edition of *Totentanz* in the Eulenburg pocket scores point to the fact that much of Liszt's music is nowadays played at overheated speeds. The last thing Liszt deserves is bravura for its own sake. Likewise, he should be shielded from anything that sounds perfumed, or what used to be called effeminate. Wilhelm Kempff's 1950 recording of the *First Legend* ('St Francis of Assisi Preaching to the Birds') presents us with poetic Liszt playing of unsurpassed quality.

LOVE Are there musicians who do not love music? I am afraid so. Are there performers who do not love the composer? You bet. The composer is our father. A performer who doesn't love his father, and obstructs his intentions and wishes on principle, should become a composer himself.

Are there pianists who do not love the piano? Does a lion-tamer love his lions? Or the trainer of a flea-circus his fleas? I love the piano as a Platonic idea, and those pianos that get close to it.

At the end of a recital in Ballarat, one of the chilliest places in Australia, I told the public that I'd like to have an axe to destroy their concert grand. Ballarat, by the way, is worth the trip. It offers an impressive showpiece of naive architecture, a cottage whose facade, garden and fence are decorated with fragments of teapots.

Our love of pieces that we play may, and should, exceed the frame of the purely structural. Colour, warmth, ardour and sensuous beauty will turn the musical love-object into a living being, as long as its tangibility doesn't motivate the executant to provide it with bruises and haemorrhages.

Of the seventeen kinds of love, number sixteen is the rarest. It hides, like the Australian lyre-bird, in the thicket of forests. But it exists.

M

MARKINGS The composer has taken the trouble to provide us with markings: evidently, they appeared important enough to him. Markings are there to be noticed by the player. Whoever thinks that they are cursory or superfluous should study the recapitulation of the Adagio in Beethoven's 'Hammerklavier' Sonata and absorb every detail in order to get the measure of the exactness, sensitivity, and meticulous care of Beethoven's imagination.

There are, to be sure, open questions and misunderstandings. After the second Arioso ('Ermattet, klagend') and the 'reawakening of the heartbeat' (Edwin Fischer) on the tenfold-repeated G major chord in Beethoven's A flat major Sonata, Op. 110, the inversion of the fugue begins. It is marked *l'istesso tempo della fuga poi a poi di nuovo vivente* ('The same tempo of the fugue gradually coming to life again'). The inner programme of this movement that has led us from the *Arioso dolente* and the 'Exhausted lament' to the gradual return to life indicates that this return does not signify a continuous accelerando – as played for instance by Solomon – but a process within the composition. Taking up its basic tempo once more, the fugue is being, *di nuovo*, revived.

The same markings can, as we know, mean different things with different composers. Few masters have written down the essential as suggestively as Beethoven did. Mozart's markings range from complete absence to superabundance. Schubert's, in his piano works, are at times less complete and conclusive than in his chamber music. His long stretches of *pianissimo* followed by a number of diminuendos are well known; here, the intermediate dynamic steps that would make such diminuendos feasible are missing, and it is left to the player to supplement them. Chopin modified his markings again and again. Brahms and Liszt (notably in the B minor Sonata) communicate, like Beethoven, the essential. Busoni under-marked while the instructions of Reger, Schoenberg, Berg and Ligeti border on the excessive. The genius of precision and practicality was Bartók.

It is supremely important that in Beethoven and Schubert – and elsewhere – *pp* and *p* should be clearly distinguished: as volumes of sound no less than in their different character. Schubert's *pp espressivo* inhabits a wider lyrical area than Beethoven's *pp misterioso* (more rarely: *pp dolce*), to use Rudolf Kolisch's familiar distinctions. Moreover, the difference between *f* and *ff* should always be clearly discernible. An acute awareness of dynamic terraces and events will enable an approach to music that translates it, as it were, into geography and makes us perceive a piece like a landscape, with mountains and valleys, citadels and ravines

– not forgetting the sensation of distances, of near and far. In the variations of Beethoven's Op. 111 the mental image will extend to the subterranean and stratospheric.

METRONOME I do not belong to the league of musicians who unquestioningly accept the metronome markings of great composers. The tempo minim = 138 for the first movement of the 'Hammerklavier' Sonata is precipitate (Beethoven wrote to his publisher: 'the assai has to go'), while quaver = 92 for the Adagio is surely too fluent. Schumann's 'Träumerei' at crotchet = 100 has no chance to dream, and some of Schoenberg's metronome indications in his Piano Concerto are simply unplayable. The most sensible markings of any composer I know are Bartók's – yet in his recording of his Suite Op. 14, he plays three of the four movements substantially faster than indicated.

What David Satz, Rudolf Kolisch's assistant, wrote *à propos* Kolisch's essay 'Tempo and Character in Beethoven's Music' seems to me essential: 'For Kolisch as for any other serious musician, tempo was only one aspect of performance; no element of performance was to be neglected at the expense of another.' Only after all elements of performance have been taken into account can the tempo be determined.

MOVED, AND MOVING C. P. E. Bach said that only the musician who is himself moved can move others. In contrast, Diderot and Busoni claimed that actors or musical performers who set out to move others must not themselves be moved, in order not to lose control. Let us try to be moved and controlled at once.

MOZART Grand master of opera, the piano concerto, the concert aria and the string quintet. His piano sonatas seem to me, with few exceptions, underrated. Artur Schnabel has splendidly summed up why: they were too easy for children and too difficult for artists. For the most part, the sounds they suggest are those of a wind divertimento; others, like the famous A major Sonata K331 and the C minor Sonata K457, are distinctly orchestral. So, too, is the C minor Fantasy K475. Orchestral versions of the two latter works emerged soon after Mozart's death. Mozart's relatively rare works in minor keys are particularly precious: the A minor Rondo K511 and the B minor Adagio K540 are soliloquies of the most personal kind. Stupendous in their chromatic boldness are the Minuet K355/576b and the Gigue K574. Wagner admired Mozart as a great chromaticist.

Mozart – to quote myself – is made neither of porcelain, nor of marble, nor of sugar. The cute Mozart, the perfumed Mozart, the permanently ecstatic Mozart, the 'touch-me-not' Mozart, the sentimentally bloated

Mozart must all be avoided. An important key to Mozart playing is operatic singing.

The grown-up Mozart said what he intended to say with a perfection rarely encountered in compositions of the highest order. More commonly, the minor masters smooth out what may sound rugged, bold or odd in the music of their great precursors. In Busoni's beautiful 'Mozart Aphorisms' we find the sentence: 'Along with the riddle, he presents us with its solution.'

N

NOTATION Being able properly to read, and grasp, the written text of a composition ranks among the performer's supreme skills. The difficulty of the task should not be underestimated. Besides taking in the written letter the performer needs to put it into practice.

However, the necessary execution does not always conform with the printed page. Here are three examples.

1. The adjustment of dotted rhythms to triplets in the baroque manner has remained alive in Schubert's music, but also on occasion in Chopin's and Schumann's. A glance at the autographs – in the case of Schubert's 'Wasserflut' from *Winterreise*, also at the first printing – makes this clear. Beethoven's notation was more literal and modern. In the C sharp Adagio of his so-called 'Moonlight' Sonata the semiquaver of the principal voice 'has to follow the last triplet below', as Czerny remarks.

2. In the recitatives of Mozart's operas, two repeated notes should not be sung as written but rather as appoggiaturas with a raised, or, more rarely, lowered, first note.

3. Among the most frequent examples of the incorrect application of textual fidelity, there is one that concerns pianists only. We can distinguish between sounds

that are written down to the letter and others that are imagined and have to be supplemented with the help of the pedal. The Viennese piano teacher Josef Dichler called them 'musical' and 'technical' notations. In the musical one, the actual duration of sound matches exactly that of the written score. The technical one, on the other hand, needs to employ the services of the pedal because it merely shows how long the finger(s) can or should stay on the key, whereas the notes themselves should continue to sound. For the first bars of the 'Hammerklavier' Sonata, Beethoven offers the necessary pedal marking; frequently, however, the use of the pedal seemed so obvious to the composer that markings are missing.

The composer who possibly suffers most is Schubert. His piano writing appears fragmentary if the pedal does not orchestrate it at the necessary places, and warm it up. A work like the first movement of the unfinished C major Sonata ceases, without sufficient pedal, to make any sense to me. Schubert's bass notes must often be held by the pedal even if marked with staccato dots where the left hand has to instantly leave the key. Of course there are cases where the player has to decide whether 'technical' or 'musical' treatment is appropriate.

For any pianist, the use of the best *Urtext* editions ought to be mandatory. Wherever possible we should, in addition, consult the original sources. Where the text is incomplete, as sometimes in Mozart, we are entitled to complement and ornament – in proper style.

O

OCTAVES are frequently played as if containing a main voice at the top and an accompanying voice at the bottom, and usually vice versa in the left hand. As a result, the sound of the fifth fingers easily gets emphasised.

I like to hear octaves as a unity, as a new colour provided by *one* instrument. The heightened attention that goes to the thumb results in a warmer sound. Octaves in the bass are mostly to be treated as alterations of colour and not as doublings that should boost dynamics. To pound out left-hand octaves is a frequent mistake.

In fast virtuoso octaves, the player has to prove that he stays in control of the musical situation. Some pianists, for whom fast octaves present no problems, seem possessed by a special devil that propels them to simply take off. In double octaves, as in Tchaikovsky's B flat minor Concerto, the temptation to show off is considerable as well. Instead of giving the music weight and emphasis, they appear to run wild.

ORCHESTRA Nothing could be more gratifying for a pianist than to feel a high-class orchestra on his or her side, an orchestra that listens with open ears, breathes the same breath, and joins the music in sympathy. The sound of the orchestra, the multitude of its timbres, the scope of its dynamics, but also its rhythmic discipline are, for our playing, the required reference point. The other supreme model is singing, the human voice, the connection between singing and speaking.

Great conductors can demonstrate to us what an orchestra is capable of, how one deals with it, which nuances of tempo may be suggested and demanded. Piano music of an orchestral character was not an invention of Romanticism. As early as Bach and Mozart, orchestrally inspired movements can be found, while Haydn in his late E flat Sonata suddenly turns towards an orchestral style. Among Mozart's piano sonatas, there are also some that clearly indicate an orchestral imagination. In his A minor Sonata K310, the first movement is symphonic, the second a soprano aria with a dramatic middle section, while the third can be easily identified as wind writing. A majority of Mozart's sonatas share this predisposition for the sound of wind instruments. Schubert, not only in his *Wanderer Fantasy* but also in most of his sonatas, was firmly on the side of the orchestra. And in Schumann's *Symphonic Etudes*, the frustrated piano virtuoso conjured up an orchestra in his own personal manner, unleashing all of the instrument's orchestral glories.

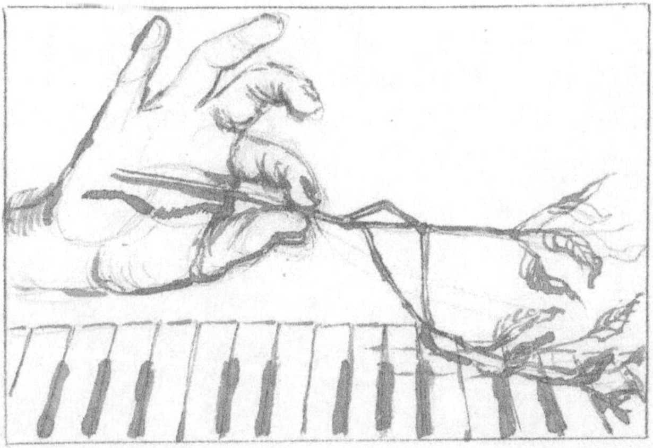

P

PEDAL The pedal belongs exclusively to the piano – I am not concerned here with the organ or the harp – and is our most precious and personal artistic tool. I am speaking, of course, of the right pedal, that sustains the sound up to the next change of pedalling but also reacts to the most minute pedal vibrations. In addition, the pianos of Beethoven's time provided the so-called *Pianozug* that reduced soft playing to a ghostly whisper. On Biedermeier pianos, one could find half a dozen pedals; one of them, the cymbal-crash pedal, would have made Mozart laugh if he could have employed it in his *Rondo alla turca.*

There are laymen and purists who believe that the pedal mostly serves the purpose of concealing bad technique and placing the sound under water, echoing the admonitions of one's earliest piano teacher. If used expertly, the pedal creates colour and atmosphere, adds warmth and declamation to the singing line, and makes the notes, written as shorter note values because the fingers cannot, or must not, hold them, continue to sound. Without the pedal, many compositions would be virtually disfigured. Many of Schubert's works require sustained voices in the background or a third dimension of depth in their sound. Good pedalling also boosts the volume: where it needs to be increased, the sound, as a rule, ought to appear widened and not sharpened.

The pianist who plays 'into the pedal' often needs to employ a different kind of articulation. His own ear – including the inner one – will be the mobilising and controlling instance. Passages in the lower part of the piano generally tolerate less pedal while the treble of a Steinway yearns for it.

Although Liszt tended, in his pedal markings, to be rather cursory, and left a work like the B minor Sonata without any pedal indications, dealing with his piano compositions gives us incomparable insight into the pedal's body and soul. One of the greatest masters of the pedal I had the good fortune to hear was Wilhelm Kempff.

(*See also* SOFT PEDAL.)

PERFORMANCE I Broadly speaking, I see the art of interpretation as a cabinet of distorting mirrors. We perceive something. This perception already is interpretation. When we become aware of this, we are interpreting – always presupposing a degree of curiosity – the interpreted.

We look at a picture, say Giorgione's so-called *Three Philosophers* in Vienna. Some of us will concentrate purely on the painting, on the miracle of colour and composition, balance and spatial depth. Others will ask: who are these people? Why are they supposed to be philosophers? What does the picture really represent? Still others will look for clues pointing to the period around 1500. What does the naked woman in Giorgione's *La Tempesta* or Manet's *Breakfast* signify? Is there a riddle with a concealed solution? A dream image? Male fantasy? Provocation?

In music, the situation is somewhat different. A picture, a sculpture, a novel – is *there*. We can view the object, walk around the sculpture, read the book. We can also read a score and hear the music in our imagination. But few of us will be able to do this. Therefore music requires interpreters for its performance – hence its kinship to the theatre. Paul Klee thought of himself as a 'complete dramatic ensemble'. Let us follow his example.

A few performers hold the view that music only begins to live when it is being turned into sound. No, she is, to a large extent, already alive in the score. But she is dormant. The performer has the privilege of rousing her or, to put it more lovingly, of kissing her awake.

PERFORMANCE II *How much in this world depends on execution becomes evident when we consider that coffee drunk from wine glasses turns out to be a rather dismal drink, or meat cut at the table with scissors, or even, as I once observed myself, butter spread on bread with the help of an old, if spotlessly clean, shearing knife.*

(Johann Christoph Lichtenberg, *Sudelbücher*, L, 501)

PERFORMER Well before Hegel, it was known that people consist of contradictions. The performer is a prize example. His playing is aimed at the composer as well as at the audience. He must have an overview of the whole piece, yet, at the same time, allow it to emerge from the moment. He follows a concept, yet lets himself be surprised. He controls himself and forgets himself. He plays for himself and for the remotest corner of the hall. He impresses by his presence and, at the same time, if luck is on his side, dissolves into the music. He reigns and serves. He is convinced and critical, believer and sceptic. When the right wind blows, interpretation presents the synthesis.

According to an ancient definition, rhetoricians should educate, move and entertain. The performer is a rhetorician. He should set standards and not play down to the public. He should move but not present his emotions on a platter. And he should not shy away from being cool and light, funny and ironic where the music calls for it.

PIANO A glance at the scope and wealth of piano literature makes us realise: this instrument works wonders. But the piano must be an instrument, not a fetish. It serves a purpose. Without the music, it's a piece of furniture with black and white teeth. A violin is, and stays, a violin. The piano is an object of transformation. It permits, if the pianist so desires, the suggestion of the singing voice, the timbres of other instruments, of the orchestra. It might even conjure up the rainbow or the spheres. This propensity for metamorphosis, this alchemy, is our supreme privilege.

To accomplish it we need an instrument of superior quality. What may the discerning pianist expect? The piano should have an even sound from treble to bass, and be even in timbre and dynamic volume. It should be brilliant enough without sounding short and clanky in the upper register, or drowning out the singing upper half with its lower one. The soft-pedal sound shouldn't be thin and 'grotesque' but round and lyrical, its dynamics reaching up to *mezzoforte*. Its action should be well measured in key-depth and key resistance. And it should, ideally, be suited for a concerto no less than for a Lieder recital. For the noisiest piano concertos, however, a particularly powerful concert grand may be the only answer.

There are pianists who are content just to play the piano. Their ambition stops at what the instrument has to offer if it is only played in 'the beautiful and right way'. In contrast, the most important piano composers – apart from Chopin – have not been piano specialists; they enriched music in its entirety. The piano is the vessel to which a multitude of sounds are entrusted, the more so since one single player is authorised to control the whole piece. In his solo playing, the pianist is independent of other players. But he bears sole responsibility as his own conductor and singer.

For these reasons, it is not my most pressing concern to take, for authenticity's sake, a certain harpsichord, hammerklavier or Pleyel piano of 1840 as a yardstick, simply because the composer may have favoured such an instrument. What matters more to me is to make manifest the sounds that a piano piece latently contains. The modern piano with its extensive dynamic and colouristic possibilities is well equipped to do this. The pianist should make himself acquainted with the orchestral, vocal and chamber works of the masters. A well-known musician has advised young pianists to spend two years browsing through the entire piano literature. I'd rather spend the time dealing with the *other* music the composer wrote. Such an extension of one's horizon might enable the player to differentiate the first movement of Bach's *Italian Concerto* as an orchestral piece that alternates tuttis with solos, the second as an aria for oboe and continuo, and the third, for once, as a harpsichord piece.

Concert grands of recent decades have progressively tended towards the harsh and percussive – or so it seems to me while writing this in 2012. (The great old pianists would have turned away in despair.) Pianos of the past displayed an inner resonance that gave the sound length and warmth. Yet even today it is possible to find, once in a while, a wonderful, magnificent instrument. Frequently, it has been monitored by one of the leading concert technicians. My collaborations with the finest exponents of this trade count among the happiest experiences of my musical life.

PROGRAMMES I once saw a poster for a recital that started with Beethoven's Op. 111, immediately followed before the interval by the Liszt B minor Sonata, and duly repressed the name of the pianist. It certainly is permissible to put strongly contrasting works next to one another. (I myself dared to place Liszt Rhapsodies between compositions by Bach and Beethoven's *Diabelli Variations.*) But it is surely inadmissible to open a recital with Beethoven's final sonata, a work that concludes the succession of his thirty-two sonatas and leads irrevocably into silence. The choice of such a programme shows that the player is unaware of the work's significance.

Programmes can be inspired by various practical and artistic considerations. Many possibilities are conceivable. What I would strongly urge against, however, is a succession of works in the same key – let alone a one-key evening. I once heard the two great B flat sonatas, Beethoven's Op. 106 and Schubert's D960, played one after the other, and realised that there are masterpieces that remain incompatible.

A pianist who had read my essay on musical humour devised a whole programme of funny pieces. What may have looked delightful on paper didn't work in practice.

In terms of duration, two halves of roughly forty minutes are considered the norm, but there are bound to be exceptions.

PULSE Both pulse and spine guarantee continuity. The spine provides flexible firmness, the pulse animates, yet maintains control. The awareness of the small note values in particular generates sensibly maintained rhythm, but also sensibly executed tempo modifications. A pulse in quavers (eighth-notes) will give the fugue of Beethoven's Op. 106 superior control.

Let me say once again that nearly all the great piano composers have also, or principally, been ensemble composers. Some piano soloists disregard this and mistake taut rhythmic organisation for a straitjacket. It would be more appropriate to talk about a well-tailored suit. The notion that ensemble composers would subscribe to an altogether different rhythmic ethos when composing solo pieces is, as a principle, hard to believe.

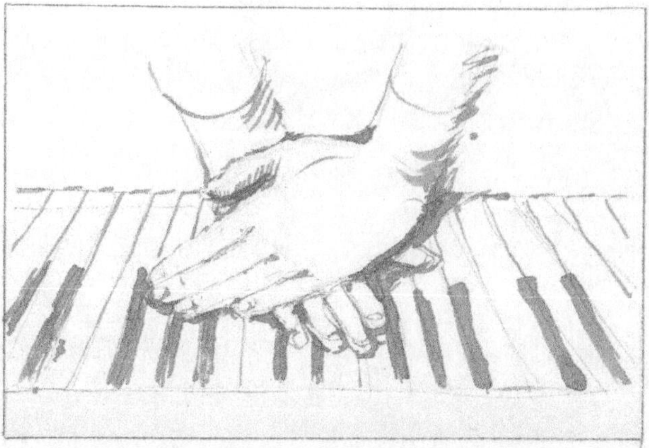

Q

QUERFLÜGEL A rare keyboard instrument, to be played diagonally, built in 1824 by Broadwood ('Traverse Piano') for the exclusive use of Prince Karl von Lobkowitz, who sported one longer and one shorter arm. The only surviving specimen, kept in the basement of Vienna's Palais Lobkowitz, bears an indecipherable dedication by Beethoven.

R

RECORDING In a BBC interview the aging ornithologist and eccentric Ludwig Koch presented for the first time a wax cylinder that had immortalised the piano playing of Johannes Brahms. Alas, all that has remained of the first *Hungarian Dance* is rasp and crackle. The recording that took place at the house of Brahms's friend Dr Fellinger had in fact been organised by an agent of the Edison Company. Ludwig Koch concluded his interview with the revelation that he was an illegitimate descendant of Napoleon – 'but it's a secret'.

Subsequently, pianos emerged that 'played all by themselves', as if operated by a ghost: the Pianola by Welte-Mignon, the creations of the Hupfeld Company (Dea, Duophonola and Triphonola), and the Ampico system. The keys and sound of the instrument were set in motion with the help of perforated paper reels. On some of these pianos, the pedal, the dynamics and the speed could be manipulated. Accustomed as we are to our present technology, we find it hard to understand how some of the erstwhile pianistic celebrities could react to the results with jubilation.

In a parallel development, records and gramophones with a horn had begun to circulate. We can now hear the voice of Vladimir de Pachmann, the clown among

Chopin players. Before starting the 'Minute' Waltz he promises to play, in the recapitulation, 'staccato *à la* Paganini' – which indeed he does.

The 1930s brought recordings of the Busch and Kolisch Quartets, the pianistic art of Fischer, Cortot and Schnabel, the by now palpable magic of Furtwängler conducting the overture to *A Midsummer Night's Dream*. Has 'technical progress' really improved the sound of piano recordings since these days? Most performances of the Busch Quartet have, for me, retained their presence as well as their plasticity. Where technical progress has undoubtedly been achieved is in the reproduction of the orchestra. This progress, however, can lead to dynamic extremes – once the distance from loud to soft ranges from a whisper to a roar, the listener will need a soundproof apartment to be able to take in such fidelity unpunished, unless he doesn't mind constantly regulating the sound, boosting the softest and scaling down the loudest as if listening to music in a car.

Record producers and sound engineers are modern magicians. They can render musicians incalculable service, and even administer, to the cheeks of a pale performance, a touch of rouge. But they can also be driven by an ambition to make every line of the score equally audible. By turning the sound into some kind of two-dimensionality they make us long to return to a good concert hall where the strings are still sitting in front of the winds and the priorities of the conductor remain respected.

REPERTOIRE It is no accident that piano music boasts the biggest solo repertoire. On the piano, one single player can 'master' the complete work with all its parts without the interference of partners. This is a bonus as well as a danger. Thanks to the complexity of the task, the development of a pianist is slower than that of violinists, who play a single voice or double-stops. While violinists can already achieve excellence in their early years, pianists will more likely reach their peak between forty and sixty. The danger consists in a high-handedness that does not do justice to musical responsibility. To be sure, piano literature will, in its more fantastic, improvisatory or recitative-like passages, present the player with the opportunity to live out his spontaneity to the full. In such situations, the inner baton comes to rest. Generally, however, our interior conductor will be the bearer of our standard. Even in comparatively unbuttoned performances, the listener should be able to write down the printed rhythm.

In planning their future, young pianists would be well advised to consider whether they want to build a comprehensive repertoire or seek specialisation. Which works are, thanks to their quality, worth spending a lifetime with? Which should we dare to take on? And which somewhat minor ones can we afford to include as a luxury? The question of musical quality will start to present itself early on. Even if we cannot assess things properly right away, we ought to attempt to divide the wheat from the chaff to the best of our abilities. Studying composition, and becoming familiar with a wide range of music, will both contribute to recognising a work's originality, its novelty within an era. During some decades the repertoire will expand, in later years it may need to be reduced. The pianist who presents important new music in an accomplished way and spreads its gospel is worthy of the highest praise.

RHYTHM Healthy, genuine rhythm remains one of the performer's supreme assets. All too readily, a soloist will enjoy the absence of the shackles imposed by ensemble playing. Unlike the case with ensemble rhythm, one can speak of soloistic rhythm in the negative. Even where, temporarily, he may permit himself more elasticity, the soloist will be well advised not to lose touch with the discipline of ensemble rhythm. Such discipline should not be mistaken for a lack of imagination or the relentlessness of a machine. It is the pulse of smaller note values that determines ensemble playing. Soloists as well will benefit from taking it to heart.

RITARDANDO In Beethoven's time, and well into the nineteenth century, there seems to have been no clear distinction between ritardando (rallentando) and ritenuto. We can deduce this from Carl Czerny's *Piano School* Op. 500 (1839). Ritardando did not necessarily suggest a gradual slowing; it could also mean that the pace had to become slower immediately. In a chart, Czerny presented a summary of cases where a slowing of the tempo is advisable even without a composer's indication. I quote from the original English version:

A ritardando may be of advantage in passages which form a return to the main subject; during the transition to a new tempo, or to a movement wholly different from the preceding one; occasionally in a heavily marked passage where a strong crescendo leads to a significant movement [?] or to the end of a piece; and finally, in almost every case, where the composer has put espressivo.

RULE, NORM Rules ask to be called into question. We should obey them only if, after thorough scrutiny, they still make normative sense, and, even then, not without reservations. A good number of ideas of articulation and declamation that have been imposed on the music will prove to be inadequate. All too easily, they iron out diversity. Among examples of fixed ideas that have become second nature to some musicians we find stereotypically played two-note groups, a penchant for diminuendos that doesn't even spare energetic endings, and the habit of executing the concluding chord only after a hiatus. Each masterpiece, each phrase is, in certain ways, a novelty. To be receptive to such diversity should be our ambition, our pride and our pleasure.

S

SCHUBERT Creator of an all-embracing world of over six hundred songs, with magnificent contributions to chamber music and the symphony. Grand master of four-hand piano music.

Schubert may well be the most astonishing phenomenon in musical history. The richness of what he accomplished in a life of merely thirty-one years defies comparison.

I should hasten to mention his two-hand piano works. With the exception of the Impromptus and *Moments musicaux*, most of them were neglected for many years. The works composed between 1822 and 1828 take us from the *Wanderer Fantasy* to the B flat Sonata. They are worthy of superlative honours. The drama of their development sections alone disproves the myth of Schubert the exclusive lyricist. In the *Wanderer Fantasy*, the piano is turned into an orchestra more drastically than had ever been attempted before. It seems almost miraculous that a composer who had not been a virtuoso player himself could display such an instinct for novel and forward-looking possibilities of piano sound and texture. All the later sonatas are orchestral in design, with the exception of the last three, which to me seem closer to the sound of a string quintet. Schubert's piano style belies the opinion that he did not add anything new to the treatment of the instrument. It has its own, highly authentic aura, an aura that, to become effective, relies on sensitive and inspired pedalling.

SCHUMANN A grand master of the Romantic piano, and the Lied. In the splendid sequence of his earlier piano works we find a special predilection for the profane reality of amusement parks and ballrooms, next to messages of love addressed to Clara. In the *Kinderszenen* we find virtuosity under the spell of Paganini next to poetic empathy with children. The orchestral piano stakes its claim: in his *Symphonic Etudes*, Schumann brings together variations, etudes and the full power of the symphonic orchestra. His *Papillons* preserve glimpses of the moment, following in the footsteps of Beethoven's *Bagatelles* op. 119, while the *Faschingsschwank* depicts the whirl of Viennese dancing. In addition, *Carnaval* exhibits a gallery of masks and portraits. In the *Humoreske*, affectionate intimacy complements the leaps and bounds of a whimsy to which the title refers. The pieces of *Kreisleriana* point by turns to Kapellmeister Kreisler (G minor) and Clara (B flat major), whereas the great C major Fantasy, in its passion and introspection, has remained 'the emblem of the piano's soul' (Edwin Fischer).

Notwithstanding the fantastic turbulence of his

music, Schumann remains a German composer. Romanticising him in a French or Russian manner leads the player astray. In a piece like the first movement of the C major Fantasy it is the quirky and passionate element in particular that cries out for a cohesive overview. Among Alfred Cortot's variable Schumann recordings from the 1930s, the *Symphonic Etudes* (apart from the finale) and *Carnaval* (apart from its introduction and conclusion) have remained unrivalled.

SILENCE is the basis of music. We find it before, after, in, underneath and behind the sound. Some pieces emerge out of silence or lead back into it.

But silence ought also to be the core of each concert. Remember the anagram: listen = silent.

SIMPLICITY According to Einstein, everything should be done as simply as possible but not 'simpler'. Inadmissible simplification and unnecessary complication are equally deplorable. This holds true for many areas of life – for a good musical performance as well as for a good newspaper. A work like Beethoven's 'Hammerklavier' Sonata should be made comprehensible without losing its complexity. 'Simple' pieces should be neither oversimplified nor over-refined. There is such a thing as fulfilled simplicity. Edwin Fischer could make it happen.

SMALL NOTES What I have in mind is not small print but smaller note values. There are musicians who lovingly execute such notes and others who tend to pass over them in favour of the longer ones, the 'main notes'. To the first group belong the Edwin Fischer Trio and Furtwängler, to the second Bruno Walter and, in units of faster notes, Artur Schnabel. I confess sympathising with the loving ones, unless the character of the music demands a lighter rhythmic treatment. Why clusters of fast notes should be lumped together I find hard to understand.

SOFT PEDAL It is not only the mechanism of hands, arms and shoulders that helps define the art of piano playing. There is also the sensitivity of our feet. The use of the left pedal extends the dynamic range down to the borders of the inaudible. The precondition: we need a very good instrument with a perfectly prepared soft pedal. I prefer pianos on which the soft pedal permits lyrical playing up to *mezzoforte*; it should encompass the whole range of Schubert's *pianissimo*.

SOUND One can play the piano (1) up from the keys, (2) into the keys, (3) out of the keys or (4) 'through the keys'. More precisely, we play in (1) not down, but up, in (2) in the direction of the lid, in (3) towards the player's body. (4) should be studiously avoided; the labelling of the piano as a percussion instrument derives from such forms of assault.

While (2) and (3) are played only incidentally, I see (1) – that is, piano playing that rises from the keys – as the foundation. Wrist and arm, shoulders and loose elbows assist the fingers. In *forte* playing in particular, a chord thrust off the keys will sound fuller and rounder than a hammered or dropped one, and an intimate contact with the keys stimulates the lyrical touch. Apart from such physical processes, sound is largely determined by balances. They have to meet the demands of character, mood and atmosphere. At the same time, sound will be defined by the awareness of voice leading, by polyphonic playing. Above all, the player should profit from the knowledge of the composers' orchestral, vocal and chamber works. The balance of a fine orchestra should remain our model.

The sound of a piano must not be taken as something absolute, but rather as a point of departure for extensive journeys, investigations of subterranean depths or flights into the stratosphere. To be sure, the player will have to cope with the acoustic circumstances and the condition of the instrument. There are halls that carry and ennoble the sound, while others adulterate it, blur it, or dry it out. There are pianos you have to make do with and others whose luminosity and soul will meet the player halfway. The saying that there are no bad pianos, only bad pianists, must have been invented by a devil operating as a piano salesman.

STACCATO In each and every case, the duration (degree of shortness) and character of the staccato have to be determined. The tones have to be separated manually, which doesn't necessarily preclude the use of the pedal. Schubert wrote *legato* ('ligato') above passages that contain staccato notes (Impromptu D935 No. 1, bar 45: *sempre ligato*, D major Sonata D850, second movement, beginning), and seems to suggest a cantabile that is realised with the help of the pedal. The fact that engravers frequently reproduced Beethoven's staccato markings as wedges has caused some confusion – this habit has been maintained in too many *Urtext* editions, to the regret of this particular customer. As a result, staccato in Beethoven can sound like a battalion of woodpeckers at work. At the beginning of Liszt's B minor Sonata there are syncopated octaves that are marked with wedges. But they are not meant to sound short and dry; according to the tradition passed on by Lina Ramann's *Liszt-Pädagogium*, they should resemble muffled timpani strokes.

Portato excludes shortness; the separation of tones is minimal if, when pedalled, it happens at all. *Portato* on repeated notes suggests a legato of the tone with itself, a tenuto cantabile. When repeated notes are unmarked it needs to be determined how long they should be played; they might as well be short, as at the beginning of Mozart's Piano Concerto K453.

SYNCOPATIONS should not sound like average notes. As they reach into the next rhythmical unit, their unwieldiness has to be made audible. Each syncopated note carries emphasis, a greater degree of emphasis than other notes of the same duration. There is a special movement for such notes that pushes the wrist gently in the direction of the piano lid.

T

TEMPERAMENT The Austrian theatre critic Alfred Polgar characterised an actor by saying that he could, with the same ease, find and lose himself. In both cases, and in all emotional situations in between, the self-monitoring function within the player must remain switched on.

TEMPO I distinguish between metronomic, psychological and improvisatory time. The metronomic one applies to certain dances and other pieces of a strict character. In the psychological one, tempo modifications appear to be so natural that we get the impression of a piece 'remaining in time', while improvisatory tempo should be deployed in passages resembling fantasy, recitative or cadenza. The music of Chopin, and sometimes that of Schumann or Liszt, calls for greater freedom. With few exceptions, Chopin's works are written for the piano alone. We shouldn't forget that his rhythmic gamut reaches from the strictest (C minor Prelude) to the freest. The basic tempo of a piece can only be determined once the performer has taken into account all its components: tempo indications, characters, dynamics, articulation, rhythmic subdivisions and pianistic feasibility. Only then can metronome markings, if there are any, be considered and, when necessary, modified.

TOUCH There may be players for whom touch and assault are synonymous. (In German, we find the deplorable word *Anschlag*, to strike.) The pianist can indeed assault the piano and, for good measure, the composer and the public. To languages that propose a more loving vocabulary, like touch and *touché*, we owe a debt of gratitude.

To avoid misunderstandings: it is perfectly possible to play vigorously and forcefully without ramming the sound through the keys like a knife.

TRANSITION There are, as you probably recall, performers who don't notice transitions at all. Others introduce them grandly and then, instead of leading into something, start anew. Transitions are areas of transformation. Listen to Furtwängler's skill at imperceptibly embarking on transitions a number of bars ahead, or anticipating, right before it starts, the character of the second theme in Schubert's 'Great' C major Symphony by a small, masterly tempo modification!

TRILLS shouldn't sound like the ringing of one and the same doorbell. Also, they are more than decorative curling or products of a geometric imagination. Trills are often, and particularly in Beethoven, agents of musical character. They can be graceful or disquieting, mysterious or demonic, smiling or menacing, innocent or seductive. There are angels' and devils' trills.

After having said all this: trills should, to a certain degree, be organised and not completely left to chance. Beautiful trills and ornaments require technical mastery.

In his *Piano School* (1828), J. N. Hummel, the leading pianist of his day, recommends the start of a trill with the main note, and requests a suffix for each true trill! Did Beethoven write down suffixes only where he really wanted them? This sounds to me overly academic. Without being consistent, Beethoven sometimes gives us suffixes simply because they require accidentals – as in Op. 101, second movement (bar 16: suffix g–a; bar 18: g sharp–a), and in Op. 106 (see the six trills before the end of the fugue).

U

UNITY In music, the call for 'unity in diversity' has been applied to both form and character. Unity without diversity tends, in most cases, to become tiresome. Diversity without unity is lively but aimless; or at least it used to be until, in the twentieth century, so many aesthetic rules started to shift, and accidental music became one of the options. It would, however, be quite misleading to treat older music in such a random fashion. Even where the appearance of spontaneity is conveyed by the performance, we should have the impression of coherence, and completeness.

V

VARIATION Works in variation form are the performer's supreme school of characterisation. Admittedly, there are also works where the variations maintain the character of their theme. In general, however, the composer will aim for variety. The player is expected to command a veritable theatre filled with characteristic types, and to control it with assurance. But he should never lose the overview. A neatly separated, side-by-side coexistence of the variations will not be an adequate solution unless we are dealing with Bach's *Goldberg Variations*.

Variations are dependent on the structure of their theme. In his *Diabelli Variations*, Beethoven has loosened this dependence in an astonishing way. Variations may now comment on the theme, mock it, put it into question and even lead it *ad absurdum*.

Within piano music variations are of special importance. They extend from Bach's *Goldberg Variations* via Haydn's lovely double variations in F minor to the second peak, the *Diabelli Variations*. Sublime sister works that we hold in awe are the final movements of Beethoven's sonatas Opp. 109 and 111. Franz Liszt renewed the form chromatically and psychologically: his *Bach Variations* entitle the player to 'weep, lament, worry and despair' until the concluding chorale redeems the listener, and himself.

VIRTUOSITY Baffling, daredevil and unprecedented? Countless notes delivered in the shortest possible time? Thunder, zestfully unleashed? This sounds like bravura for bravura's sake. A sizeable section of the public will acknowledge it with rapture. But the Romantic etude aimed higher. Triggered by Paganini's Caprices, the technically new and unheard-of had to be counterbalanced and vindicated by musical novelty, boldness and poetry. Next to the pinnacle of Chopin's etudes, those of Schumann, Liszt and Brahms (*Paganini Variations*), as well as of Debussy, Bartók and Ligeti, give pianists the chance to prove that, in their playing, music retains the upper hand. Virtuosity, by the way, will prove to be useful even if we don't spend the majority of our working hours tackling etudes – indeed, particularly so.

Frequently, when faced with runs and fast figuration, players cannot help getting faster. There will be an involuntary speeding up in the playing of technically gifted pianists – unless their musicianship checks their fingers. Playing too fast may well be a lesser physical strain than the cultivation of a discipline that controls each single fingertip.

W

WAIL 'Prolonged plaintive inarticulate loud high-pitched cry' (*Concise Oxford Dictionary*), known to be uttered by Johannes Brahms after playing the piano at his ghostly nocturnal appearances.

X

X Conlon Nancarrow's astonishing music for player piano offers performance without interpretation. As the results are fixed, the pianist can lean back and say: 'What bliss! I don't have to break a finger.' *Canon X* is one of his finest pieces.

Y

YUCK! Exclamation of displeasure. A natural reaction to memory lapses, blurred notes and fainting fits.

Z

ZVONOMIR Legendary medieval king of the Croats. His connection to music, and to this alphabet, is, at best, peripheral.

Books by Alfred Brendel that provide further reading on music and himself:

The Veil of Order: Conversations with Martin Meyer, Faber and Faber 2002 (published in the US as *Me of All People: Alfred Brendel in Conversation with Martin Meyer*, Cornell University Press, 2002)

Alfred Brendel on Music: His Collected Essays, JR Books, 2007

Playing the Human Game: Collected Poems of Alfred Brendel, Phaidon Press, 2010